Jam

Acknowledgements

International Times, Morning Star, The North, The Rialto, Stride Magazine, Under the Radar and *Set Down: A Collaboration for Laurie Lee, Curator of Eccentricity* (Yew Tree Press, edited by Philip Rush). Nineteen poems appeared in the Knives Forks and Spoons pamphlet *Bike, Rain*. 'Lighthouse 1' was published in *Frank Freeman's Dancing School* (Salt; KFS) and is included here as part of a sequence. I am grateful for an Arts Council England Grant for the Arts.

Jam
Cliff Yates

smith|doorstop

Published 2016 by
smith|doorstop books
The Poetry Business
Bank Street Arts
32-40 Bank Street
Sheffield S1 2DS
www.poetrybusiness.co.uk

Copyright © Cliff Yates 2016

ISBN 978-1-910367-55-1

Cliff Yates hereby asserts his moral right to be identified as the author of this book.

British Library Cataloguing-in-Publication Data.
A catalogue record for this book is available from the British Library.

Typeset by Utter
Printed by CPI Books / Lightning Source (USA)
Cover image: © Paul Yates
Author photo: Gillian Yates

smith|doorstop is a member of Inpress, www.inpressbooks.co.uk. Distributed by Central Books Ltd., 99 Wallis Road, London E9 5LN.

The Poetry Business receives financial support from Arts Council England

Contents

Part 1

11 Life Studies
12 Alt St Johann
13 Easter
14 The Chinese Girls Played Cards
15 Bike, Rain
16 Recession as Street Theatre
17 Boat
18 Spade Bucket Apple
19 Blackpool North
20 I Met my Friend
21 February, Colden Valley
22 Bike Ride
23 Take Heart
24 He Takes Off his Hat and Steps
25 The Chicken
26 Worb Dorf
27 You always thought you liked dogs, but your neighbour's
28 Dog-speak
29 There's a Horse in the Beech Tree
30 Just Before You Taste It
31 Shakespeare and Company

Part 2

34 Bar Billiards
35 Square Neck
36 Box

37	Lucky Jim
38	Fifteen
39	Heidelberg
40	Radford Avenue
41	The Bowling Green
42	At the Funeral
43	Chapter Twenty: Leonard Cohen
44	Jesse James
45	Glastonbury
46	The Sun Comes Out, the Radio Comes On
47	We Didn't Go to the Cinema in Those Days
49	Born in Handsworth
50	Brum
51	There's a Full-Size Snooker Table in the YMCA Furniture Shop
52	*from* Riversound
54	One More Time

Part 3

57	First Names
59	The Lesson
60	Jam Bush
61	Snails
62	Lighthouse 1
63	Blue Sofa
64	Move
66	Pilates
67	She's Living in Spain with Italians
68	Straw
69	Lighthouse 2
70	Changing the Bed
71	Then we'll have a cup of tea and put our feet up

72	How do *you* fly in your dreams?
73	Gate
74	The End of the World Again
75	Rain on the Conservatory Roof
76	The House is Almost Empty
77	Lighthouse 3
79	Everyone Took What They Wanted
80	Travis Perkins

For Thomas, Luke and Ruth

Part 1

Life Studies

I meet Tom for soup & sandwiches at Euston,
it still looks good, his twenty quid haircut, then I take
the Hammersmith & City to Goldhawk Road.
Someone said the best moments are moments
of realisation. On the bumping underground
I read *Life Studies* for the first time
since the seventies in my old Faber Selected (45p)
signed and dated with my younger signature.

O'Hara wasn't keen on Lowell and I love O'Hara
but there's something in Lowell that I recognise.
I recognise these underground stations
their names though I've never been here before.
That song by Gerry Rafferty with the unforgettable sax ...

I sit next to a girl who smells like a bag
of crisps or maybe I can just smell crisps.
It's not a girl I realise, it's a boy
with dreadlocks eating a pear at Paddington
in a pink & white scarf, camel-coloured coat,
pinstripe trousers, red & black boots ...
'Baker Street'.

Alt St Johann

The children hide in the tree;
they whisper and laugh, the branches move.
These are the mountains, the trees
on the mountains, the rocks.
You walk and you walk
and forget that you walk.

The child climbs out of the hedge, clutching
a fistful of wheat, its roots thick with soil.
Chew the husks, taste the sweetness.
The cat sits on the cooker, gazes out on the valley,
closes her eyes and opens them.

You see only half of the moon
and mist comes out of the ground.

The cherries are finished on the tree,
the redcurrants ripe on the bush.
We sleep at the top of the house in the room
full of musical instruments. The music
enters our dreams and leaves by the gate
leaving it open.   This, I decide, is paradise
where they lend you their shoes and they fit.
It's easy to laugh, and the children walk forever,
sleep through the night in the valley of stars,
wake with the light and remember.

Easter

It's different when we go back
without the children the perspective shifts. That
pool into which they threw stones is smaller
opposite the house where pink
blossom brings out the colour of the brick,
the back garden more-or-less an open field
with occasional trees, grass trimmed, fence
broken in places. I prefer boundaries crisp
except here, this place:
swerving territory of snow light.

The wind's picked up but if you
walk you soon feel warm.
The sheep have long hair, small blank heads, horns.
The good-looking cow climbs to her feet,
back legs first, steadying, her front legs thin
and strong. She raises her tail and squeezes
a stream onto the grass.

So much guilt today you can hardly bear it
but you do and carry on.
The door slams and the source of heat.
Two women, three, and I'm here all night
making stuff, making.
Place the flowers here. Now
look through the window.

Interior, yes, and very much out there the source of light.

The Chinese Girls Played Cards

The Chinese girls played cards on the train
from Zurich to Paris. At one point it rained.
They wiped their fingers on the pith of an orange
but it was the wrong kind of orange.

It rained on the way to Paris.
The sky was Swiss German, then French
and clean like the pith of an orange.
There was no rainbow that I remember

but I remember the sky changing to French.
'Danke,' I said to the French ticket inspector
with the tattoo on his arm. I remember
his careful beard, the collection of studs in his ear.

'Danke' – after he'd thanked me in English.
How did he know I was English? From my ticket,
my manner, my clothes? *Were* they Chinese?
They were speaking in French, the cards were German.

Bike, Rain
for Robert Sheppard

We have to get to a railway station. It's raining.
    'I forgot you had a bike.'
    'I know.'
    'We could try riding two-up.'
    He laughs and says, as if reading from a book:
    'He was strangely insistent about riding two on a bicycle.'
    I try to buy a bike for the journey but without conviction. The vendor has two bikes chained up. Forty pounds.
    'That's far too much. I can pay twenty pounds or twenty-eight.'
    'I'll tell you what, I'll meet you half-way: thirty-eight pounds.'
    'That's too much. I told you: twenty or twenty-five pounds. That's all I have.'
    And we're off again in the rain, him pedalling, keeping his head down and me jogging beside him. It's quite a distance, rain or no rain.
    An old town carved out of the rock face. It's a tourist attraction. You can see how they lived in authentic colour.
    'I forgot you had a bike.'
    'I know.'

Recession as Street Theatre

On the table outside the undergound
in a cramped white cage: a long-haired 'dog'
with a man's big face, whiskers glued on:
a kennelled head, bulging red eyes and lifeless paws.

Knelt on the pavement under the table,
his head poked through as if desperate
to provoke a crowd he despises
he's whistling, barking, bewildering children

but the crowd's down the road
you can see them from here, watching
not the sweating juggler playing with fire
or the man eating balloons with the massive speaker

but the Invisible Man on the high-backed chair
with the pinstripe suit, collar and tie,
his glasses and bowler wobbling in the air
and huge white gloves doing all the talking –

pointing, beckoning, silently clapping,
the invisible mute of Covent Garden.

Boat

In the morning she found a boat marooned on her pillow

she couldn't hear the survivors
she couldn't hear the sea.

The boat on the back of her hand, the size of a shell, and light.

She glimpsed it again through a window at work
holding up the traffic on the by-pass.

She could barely hear the typewriters
for the noise of the storm
in her head ...
         more land than sea
birds and more birds, a crow
on the topmost roof, the door onto the balcony ...

The cloud-sized boat capsized in the evening sky
the wide open sky, everything piled beneath it.

She rocked and she rocked asleep and awake
      to the crashing of waves.

Spade Bucket Apple

No longer one to call a spade a spade
he calls it bucket or apple, it's exhausting

like mistaking a pig for a favourite cow
then trying to milk it in a ruined building.

Blackpool North

Four rugby shirts walk downwind,
down the carriage, loaded with bags,
two of them singing.
My mate there, down the car!
Are you all right my old buddy?

Celebration and rain, the train pulls
away, the smell of beer and sandwiches
in a red scarf and hat.
It's only a loan, it's only a loan,
in eighty-three we'll bring it home.

Flat land. A pale blue shed, white
lettering. In the sky, a silver cow.
New trees in plastic tubes
and sheep facing the same direction.
and sleep facing the same direction.

I Met my Friend

I dreamed I met my friend
soon after he died,
down by the lake.
It was as if he was expecting me.
He had lost thirty years,
was in his twenties,
and had travelled further.
We stood together
leaning on the wall, gazing out.
The sun rippled on the water.
It's good, so good to see him again,
to be with him by the lake.
The sound of the water, distant
traffic, and a heron *Look, John!*
at the far end.

February, Colden Valley

The old mill chimney, brushed by a track of snow,
points to a house on the hill obscured by trees:
bare trees against cloud, blue sky. Birdsong.
River sound runs through the valley.

Beech branches, twigs against sky.
Black, silver-grey on powder blue.
Green trunk old beech, old green
evergreen, part-shade, part-sun.
One mast, framed. Lines of soft grey,
white cloud, sky the palest blue.
Land folds into valley, distant hills.

Bright moss in sunlight on the dry stone wall,
bright green feathery underwater green.
Gathered damp the stone's coat.
Sycamore seeds, last year's rested here
and leaves: gold-faded khaki, black,
stuck to frozen snow. And these –
upright purple stems with bean-shaped heads.

Bike Ride

All four of us for once, in single file
on the Birmingham Road, past the fields
on our left, the black and white cottage
and the right turn under the railway bridge.

It's surprisingly dark cycling under the bridge
when Dad moos like a cow for the echo.
There's no way he wouldn't have done that,
mooed like a cow for the echo, cycling under the bridge.

Take Heart

Two pain-killers first thing, a black tea
with three sugars and I'm almost human,
the tooth a dull ache and the throat
a mere crackle. Cheer up, says the *Express*,
forget the economy – temperatures
in the 70s, sales in the High Street

and my body's a wire, strung across the Pennines
sat in a draught on the Transpennine Express.
No one talking, just the rustle of paper,
a slate-blue sky, shadows getting shorter
as we enter a tunnel, then it's a mist
and the presence of trees, the sun
inching up the absence of sky.

Telegraph poles are poor imitations of trees;
the wires between them, bird flight.

He Takes Off his Hat and Steps

He takes off his hat and steps off the train,
looks up at the sky, puts his watch back an hour.
He reckons one day he'll be buried at sea.
His suit's wet through, he's been swimming again.

He buys a paper, leaves the change on the counter,
picks up the morning then puts it back down.
The sea's a coin under an open sky
it's always like this at the end of September.

Every morning we start over again,
come round quietly, make up the bed,
before it gets dark put the clocks back an hour
and in the morning put them forward again.

You don't need papers for the open sea,
you don't need a ticket for where we're going.
A box and a prayer, a flag and salt water,
our hats on our laps we'll sleep on the train.

The Chicken

The chicken roosts in my hair, keeps my head
dry in the rain. She broods, lays eggs that roll
down my face and when I don't catch them,
smash at my feet. She clucks in queues, on the bus.

There are rumours ... People are watching,
whispering, following us down the street,
roasting potatoes, mixing sage and onion.
Her feet clench, scratch my scalp. Something
warm runs down my neck, inside my collar ...

Mr Jenkins, out the back on the step,
honing his carving knife, nods hello over the fence.

Worb Dorf

The dimmer switch is stuck on dim
and everything's made out of wood:
creaking floor, walls, ceiling. The bed
is a box with no lid. Rain hammers

the window, the glass roof below.
It was a long night, the days
are shorter. The forecast is snow
if the rain gives it a chance.

Who is the anxious woman
in the portrait? Who are the people
downstairs, moving behind frosted glass?
In reception a man in a cap

dismantles a heater, whistling
in two languages. He seems
young in this hotel of women.
Maybe it's the same woman.

There's some confusion. She says
the same thing twice. German.
She could say it a thousand times
and I have a tram to catch.

She shows me a calendar and then
I understand. I point to Thursday,
flap my arms. She laughs. Flying
is flying in any language.

*You always thought you liked dogs, but
your neighbour's*

appears to be running at you and has just smashed
through the French windows, knocking over the milk
in the Marilyn Monroe glass that you brought back
from Slovakia; the glass is just about to hit

the tiles and the milk's like a photograph of milk
liberated from the glass, or a milk sculpture
and in the background the teeth and slavering mouth
of next door's dog, an elaborately cross-bred bitch

well over a thousand pounds and worth it
for its sociable temperament and clean habits
bearing down remarkably quickly in spite
of its replacement hip; the sun behind it

through the broken windows rising ruthlessly in a clear sky
and a jet trail refusing to vanish, making the most of it.

Dog-speak

She-boss and Big-man think they in charge
so Jake don't have crunch-taste when *he* want. No.
She-boss and Big-man put out crunch-taste
on cold-tongue and say: *Sit! Good boy! Good dog, Jake.*

Jake watch green stuff through fake-space in go-through.
Jake keep bark-watch. No smell through fake-space.
Jake watch for wing-flaps, and sly-claws who roof-walk.
Jake not roof-walk, Jake not daft, Jake stay low on hard-stuff.

Crunch-taste is good time but walk time is best time.
Jake in charge. Walk time is not just walk time.
Walk time is walk, smell, bark, run, piss, bark, shit, bark.
She-boss and Big-man shout: *Jake! Jake! Jake! Jake!*

There's a Horse in the Beech Tree

There's a horse in the beech tree
just a few days old, a colt
clinging with his legs to the branches.

If the wind picks up he will be in difficulty.

The plucky colt clings with his legs
like a spider, no safety net, no web to hang by
in September, in the breeze.

Just Before You Taste It

The best bit, she says, is just before you taste it.
Cary Grant, running through the cornfield, chased
by the crop-duster, without his jacket.
All things must pass, everything comes to an end.

Hottest day of the year and you're stuck in a carriage
missing the winning goal, the unspectacular
winning goal. Winning is always spectacular,
she says, slamming again the door.

Something's going off in the fridge, making
very little noise, making almost no noise at all.

Shakespeare and Company

We stayed in the Marais near Rue des Rosiers
on the fifth floor: ninety-two steps, toilet on the landing,
bring your own towels, €20 more than the floor below
(but what would you pay for a view of the sky?)

and bought white nectarines from the market
and baguettes from the boulangerie round the corner
from The Red Wheelbarrow, an American bookshop
like Shakespeare and Company on the Left Bank

(with the bed under the stairs) where, one night
I caught up on the history of American poetry
while the rain hammered the roof, followed by an ice-cream
from Amorino served by a girl from Hereford

who talked like an English girl in a Woody Allen film
and gave us a massive cone that we shared
by the Seine on Paris Plage, lying on deck chairs
under a sweet chestnut tree, waving at the people on boats.

Part 2

Bar Billiards

Our Christmas bar billiards is only
four foot long but it's bigger

than a playing card.
Dad says you need a

magnifying glass
to see the balls. Eyes

water in the smoke
from Uncle Fred's Woodbine

as me and my brother,
Dad and Uncle Fred

edge past each other, taking
turns in the crowded

living room, careful with our cues
(the tree, the television screen).

Mum and Aunty Alice
natter and laugh in the kitchen.

You have to start somewhere.

Square Neck

Down the hill towards the Horsefair, right
along the Stourbridge Road and it's on your left.
Forget short back and sides, ask for a square neck.
The glass case with Durex (that's where you buy them
or from the machines in the toilets at the Blue Star).

It's white coat and clippers, scissors and comb,
hair flying in your face, inside your collar,
back of your throat
                        and next day in school
keep your cap on or they'll all be after you,
including your mates, their own caps rolled up,
peaks tucked in, hitting you on the head
with them: *Hair-cut! Hair-cut!* like a truncheon.

Box

I lean against the door to open it, edge in
sideways, put the box down by the coat stand.
'I'm going to forget this box.'

The barber turns round, the lad having his hair cut
looks over his shoulder, the bloke on the sofa
puts down his paper and all four of us look at my box.

'I'll remind you,' the barber says.
The bloke on the sofa hands me a paper
and I turn to the back, to the football

to the sound of scissors and comb. The barber
hands you a tissue for the back of your neck.
'Just throw it down there,' she says.

Lucky Jim

In a box in the attic, my old copy of *Lucky Jim* –
I sit reading it on a rolled-up rug ...

Swansea, the flat above the shoe shop
on the High Street (my third of the year)
the middle of winter, teaching practice

and the caretakers' strike –
                              cold and wet
(it's always raining in Swansea) and every day
is stolen time – endless mugs of tea, bread and jam
sitting on the floor, back against the radiator,
now and then laughing out loud ...

Three years after the printing factory, a lifetime,
I'm at the back in History of Art, a Rauschenberg
projected on the screen, condensation on the windows
and my jeans steaming after the walk here
along the beach in the rain.

Fifteen

Philip Austin was born middle-aged:
Brylcreem and cycle clips, a faint moustache,
like somebody's dad, or one of the teachers.
Here he is in the bike shed, chaining up his RSW,
fifteen years old in his prefect's blazer.

Prefects. Roger gave us twenty-five lines
for mucking about, then we talked him out of it.
I saw him recently, called in at the farm.
He told me how they found their dad
in the cowshed. That's how he wants to go.

The barn I creosoted when I was fifteen
is still standing and hasn't been creosoted since.
Their Cedric showed me how to drive.
We followed a track round the edge of a field.
He had to turn off the radio. A good record
made me go faster, I didn't realise. It still does.

They'll never make me a prefect –
the special blazer, the badge – not in this lifetime,
hanging about the bike sheds, waiting for something
to happen, or singing along in the outside lane, eighty-five, ninety.

Heidelberg

Mac runs past, a Woodbine
hanging from his lips, ash
on his foreman's white overall,
his face red, sweating. Brian
catches my eye, shakes his head.
It's only nine o'clock.
I set up the Heidelberg, load
the envelopes, roll a cigarette.
Bill the Cutter's half
a finger is giving him grief.
'How's it going Bill?'
'Mind your own business.'
I hum something from *Basket of Light*
then 'Get Back' comes on the radio.
I can see Barry, daydreaming
about motorbikes,
on his bench a cartoon
of Himmler in a butcher's apron
shouting with a cleaver.
I've nicked his Stanley knife.
I'm negotiating with Neville
for the moped that I will wreck
one night on Habberley Estate.
I don't signal, take the force
of the bumper with my leg
turning right with rain
in my eyes.

Radford Avenue

I park the moped at the end of the entry
by the door to the garden and my great
grandfather's shed, and help my mother
balance the table on the back of her bike

then we wheel it home between us, laughing
up the hill, not noticing the couple in the car
with the children in the back: it's me and Gill
twenty years on, reversing badly into the one

remaining space outside St George's Park
where me and Mike turned the tramps on
in our lunch hour, sitting on the bench
by the bowling green.

The Bowling Green

The bowling green.
The shelter by the bowling green.
The benches in the shelter overlooking the bowling green.
The knocking of the balls from the bowling green.

The bowling green waiting for the bus.
The bowling green climbing aboard
the number seven. The bowling green
looking for the bus fare, searching
for loose change in its deep deep pockets.

The number seven accelerating for the hill
heading out of town. The bowling green
looking out of the window at the benches in the shelter.
The knocking of the balls from the bowling green.

At the Funeral

You don't recognise me, he said,
do you? It didn't help that he'd changed
his name. White moustache,
round red face – how was I to know?

All the lights were on
and I felt this great wave.
Everyone was smiling
and the day went on and on.

I caught a glimpse of where the dead go.
There was a great deal of space
on either side. You could tell
what was coming then it started to snow.

Chapter Twenty: Leonard Cohen

is on Mount Baldy, brewing coffee
at 3am, smoking, before the chanting
and meditation.

                Here in Lumb
after midnight the snow is gone
the valley full of wind and rain
the crescent moon over the hill.
The dead are here in the shadows.
They are not calling out or trying
to communicate, they're not
drawing attention to themselves.

The bathroom light clicks on
and the extractor fan. It's Chris
in the next room. A couple of minutes
and the fan goes off.

                Leonard Cohen's
jeep on the monastery drive, the engine
cold. It's way below zero. In a few hours
he'll be in town with the beautiful nun:
two black robes, two shaved heads
in the winter sun.

Jesse James

We met an American in Amsterdam
who spoke Dutch but the Dutch
would only answer in English
because he was American.
He said his name was Jesse James.

Jesse said yes he knew the score
a bar with the stuff laid out on a table
carefully weighed in plastic bags.
The dealer's eyes went right to left.
He said his name was Jesse James.

Everyone talking music loud
but the bar as quiet as death.
Out on the street, side of the canal
the girl on the bike, the moon on the water.
He said his name was Jesse James.

Next morning Graham shaved off his beard.
That's funny, I said, I've decided to grow one.
Hitchhiking hours out of Amsterdam
we're stranded, side of the road.
He said his name was Jesse James.

Graham was pale, he'd sat in the front,
held off the driver's wandering right hand
with our sandwiches. Here,
I said, it seems a pity to waste them.
He said his name was Jesse James.

Glastonbury

on a bench outside the Crown
a man takes a photo of his pint – the flash
lights up the street, lights up

the smell of weed
downwind from Burns the Bread
and in the Galatea, the waiter

gives me a knife and fork
for my soup instead of a spoon
as the child says, *I know the biggest*

planet, what's the furthest one called?
Her father demonstrates
with the sugar bowl, plates,

two chairs, he grabs a table,
backs it out of the door, cutlery
clatters on the pavement

and above the car park, the silhouette
of the abbey, the moon behind cloud,
the invisible scaffolding.

The Sun Comes Out, the Radio Comes On

I said you look amazing. She said I know I look forward to waking up. I said we're going to be very late do you want yours boiled or fried? She said neither and turn the telly off before you burn something. I said what happened to the curtains?

I stay home instead of come with you to your mother's because I have work to do but what do I do exactly? I finish off the biscuits with the paper, the dishwasher going and our lad upstairs working on his art and think I hear the vacuum cleaner he must be cleaning his room having tidied it that's unusual but the vacuum cleaner's downstairs, I checked, so it's my hearing. We had snow earlier and hail but not for long.

We threw down our coats and bags by the door. In the night I mistook them for a sleeping dog, and your toilet bag, left on the cupboard, for a trilby.

We Didn't Go to the Cinema in Those Days

1. Wardrobe

Overhead, my companions
the coat-hangers knock together
when the door opens, reminders
of the clothes that hung here.

The smell of clothes has long gone.
The only smell is wardrobe.
There's a drawer down below.
Maybe someone sleeps in the drawer

but if they do, I can't hear them.
There's a shelf above the coathangers.
A top hat once lived there with a story to tell.
I'd listen to his story over and over

his voice as deep as the black of his silk.
I don't remember a word he said.

2. Iceberg

Inside the iceberg, weightless,
ice at my back, underfoot, pressed
on my chest, face, I watch the stars
come and go, blue sky, ocean.
Ice blood in veins. No space

for my hair to grow, eyes to close.
Nowhere to go. I dream that, melting,
paper-thin, it cracks and ice-water runs
down my face, I catch my breath, lungs
expand, gurgle, bubble ... No.

Ships pass, point me out. Tourists.
Best-kept secret. Look children,
a man in the ice, trapped, kept fresh.
Old-fashioned clothes. See his face, light
in his eyes. He can see us. He's alive.

3. Steeple

I lean against the steeple
two hundred feet above the ground.
A pigeon lands on my head.
The fire brigade have gone.
No more children throwing stones.

As thin as the spire and completely still
I forget to breathe and rarely sleep.
I like it best when the sun goes down.
I stare at the stars like I'm one of them.
I forget who I am.

Born in Handsworth

Your blowlamp eyes are Soho Road
that see as far as Perry Barr.
Your hair is Yardley Wood, your head
Barr Beacon, your gut the spiral
of Spaghetti Junction. Your arteries
are the canal or maybe the Rea.

The crick in your neck is Kingstanding,
the Bull Ring a navel piercing,
your vertebrae the Jewellery Quarter.
Your belly's Digbeth, your brain Five Ways.
Your spinal fluid's rain, just rain
on Lickey Hills, on Cannock Chase,
your beating heart is Villa Park.

Brum
for Andrew Taylor

I'm due into New Street at 12.14 and Andy at 12.10
and it's me waiting for him at the barrier.
It's lunch in the Custard Factory near the oldest
pub in Brum, we could stay all afternoon but the sun
is out so we head for the cathedral other side the station.
The teachers are on strike, we check out their demo
in Victoria Square, chat to a couple of coppers
just out of short trousers with nothing to do:
'You don't have to wear ties then, these days?'

Then it's the John Salt at the Ikon and
a coke under the white parasols.
Down by the canal heading back into town
there's a couple on a narrow boat
we watch from the bridge. He's steering,
leaning into the bend motorbike-style, one eye
on his girlfriend who's checking her mobile.
They nearly lose the umbrella in the breeze but there
he is! up on the roof rescuing it then back on the tiller:
'It's OK love, I'll take over.'

There's a Full-Size Snooker Table in the YMCA Furniture Shop

I stand there for ages looking at it, thinking
how wonderful to have one, to have the room
for a full-size snooker table, the colours
of the balls against the green, the way they snap,
the sound when you pot one, the paraphernalia
of scoring, the everlasting cube of blue chalk ...

I hand over a wad of notes and a couple
of lads help me manoeuvre the snooker table
out of the door. They watch me ease it
onto my shoulder and head off home in the rain,
pockets bulging with snooker balls, the cues
strapped to my back like a quiver of arrows.

from *Riversound*
In which Kevin learns to breathe out of water

I'm dry, dead leaf dry. Crisp. Twig-lung.
Kindling. You could burn me. Strike a match –
vroom. The need to be underwater,
to doze, to climb out at night and sing.
Part of me sleeps. Waterworld, bubbledamp.
If only our bed could be damp.

✤

I lie in the bath, submerge. Her key in the door ...
*I'm in the bath. / You're always in the bath. /
I can't help it. / I know.* She adds more hot,
takes off her clothes, climbs in ...
She towel-dries her hair as I climb out,
pull on my shirt. *You're still wet ... / I know.*
The shirt clings to my back, jeans to my legs,
water drips down my face, down my neck.

✤

He sings in his sleep, stares into space
and sees water. We have wet towels
on radiators, water boiling in the kitchen.
Condensation streams down the walls.
I wake in the night, hear him in the bath.
I can't build the fire or he sits in the corner,
feet in a bowl, shaking. I have to watch him
in the rain, he'd take off his clothes if I let him.

⌘

I love sound in air world. Music. Air vibrates
and carries it; water muffles, wraps round.
You couldn't hear music this clear in water.
Riversound is different: lovely, but you
always hear that water is there. Bubble. Sloosh.
Above water sunlight is purer. Though air
is so thin I get dizzy. It's too easy to breathe ...

⌘

Street noise. People. Try not to catch their eye.
Remember not to stare. Do like she says:
hands in pockets, eyes on pavement ...
Sudden rain. Delicious wet. Rain on pavement,
rain on cars, streaming down the gutter,
gurgling in the drain. I stand on a corner,
eyes closed, rain on my face. She's here –
she takes my arm, pulls me along, talks,
keeps me awake so that people don't see,
people don't guess. Hair soaked, clothes.
No scarf, no hat, let it pour, soak through.
Don't wring me out, let me stay wet
so that when you touch me water comes.
Rain makes me happy and floods are a reminder.
Rainbow, moonlight on water, moon glow.

One More Time
for Mimi Khalvati

Come back to bed, she whispers in rhyme,
come back to bed, there's always more time.

Hair going grey, eyes wearing out,
nights you lose it, passing the time.

There at the end, a stranger's tent.
Days without sleep, you're a stranger to time.

Roadworks ahead, I drop down to third,
slide in a tape: *I got too much time ...*

Soldiers search the floor below,
light through curtains marking time.

The kite's caught the wind, I'm hanging on,
top of the cliff, just one more time.

Come back to bed, she whispers in rhyme,
come back to bed, there's always more time.

Part 3

First Names

1. Aardvark

big as a badger, burrows and snout
bugs for breakfast, earthpig

2. Aardwolf

blackstripe, hyena night, earthwolf
termite eater, aard as nails, tough as boots

3. Aaron's beard

rose of Sharon –
gives us a song, tender and long
her belly shining in the morning sun
haystack, a glass of apples, rose petal jam ...
Learning to shave with your father's razor
love after school by the long jump pit

4. AB blood type

potential universal recipient
beginner's blood

5. Abaca

Manila hemp, abaca abaca
sounds like a train, banana brain
grow your own filter paper, teabags, banknotes
pseudostem, Tagalog Tagalog

6. Abacus

abadust, a page of wind, a child's toy
what race? no trace, uncount, share
strung out, sunlight through glass
and every sound goes through you
lines on rock, lines on sand
lines on water, lines on air

7. Abalone

no, not the album by Roxy Music –
muttonshell, ormer, mother of pearl
ear shape, shallow shell, soundless
edible mollusc of warm seas
abalone abalone
first in line, shine

8. Abertawe

In the beginning
reading *Leaves of Grass*
on Swansea beach, time stopped –
sand in your watch

The Lesson

The nun points out the ones to watch:
the boy in the corner, the girl at the back.
In this class it's the boy in the middle
who thinks he's a cat.

Outside, workmen are felling trees.
A bird's nest tumbles in through the window,
lands on a desk. Inside the nest, a baby bird.
It's okay it's okay, the children say,
Brian will know what to do.

The boy who thinks he's a cat
gathers the bird and, holding it
at arm's length in the cup of his hands,
heads for the door, the nun behind him
between the silent rows of children
and the bird, as if on cue, lifts up its beak and sings.

Jam Bush

It grows at the end of the garden, its buds
like bells or fairy lights. Squeeze them
and the thin glass pops. Eggshell skin.

Lick your fingers. Wasps hover, sensing
the treasure, and the buds take shape –
tiny jars, lids tight, labels you can

barely read: strawberry, blackcurrant.
Leave them too long, they weigh down
the branches, sit on the ground,

labels facing the house. Apricot, damson.
Our youngest harvests them before they harden,
peels back the glass, puts the fruit on her tongue.

Snails

'I've never seen so many snails,' my wife says,
'and the slug powder's gone hard.' I take a knife
from the cutlery drawer and head for the greenhouse.

On the way, I accidentally kick over a bucket
of rainwater into which she has dropped a number
of snails, a dozen at least. I don't know, at this stage,

that she has dropped snails into the bucket,
snails which are now making their way
back to the vegetable patch. Meanwhile

I am digging at the white powder with the knife.
It is very hard. It must have got damp.
Birds are singing and the ground is wet.

Lighthouse 1

The lighthouse flickers at the end of the pier.
We watch it in our red pyjamas.
Actually neither of us are wearing red pyjamas.
You're wearing my blue shirt.

The lighthouse flickers at the end of the pier.
It's the only thing we can be sure of.
Everything's uncertain
since you set alight my record collection.

I'm trying to work out an appropriate reaction,
rearranging things in my head to eliminate
all memory of the record collection.
The lighthouse flickers on and off.

Actually it doesn't, you point out, it just appears to.
You look amazing in my blue shirt.
I haven't words to describe how good you look
in the light from the lighthouse. Now you're here

now you're not. Maybe I should burn
something of yours, you suggest.
Your voice leaves me in the dark.
It doesn't sound like you when I can't see you.

Blue Sofa

For one hour the children are young again.

I have just come in from work
and read to them on the blue sofa,

the boys either side, Ruth on my lap
turning the pages.
                    We have read this book
a hundred times and they're absorbed,
entranced by the words, the pictures ...

I'm so tired that I am nearly asleep.
The kettle boils, the windows steam.

Move

1. *Move*

A plastic starfish from the children's sandpit
was on the floor of the car for ages
before we moved, ferrying load after load
of things that would not fit in our new house

to Southport Animal Rescue, who take
anything: an old cassette player, blankets
for their dogs. We parked in the multi-storey,
fish & chips at Harper's then a walk

on the pier in the wind, the tide
always out except that one time,
when it was in and blue, the woman
singing along to a backing track

in the open air to a handful of people
sipping tea from white mugs and I am still
getting used to it or trying to: not at work and
nothing wrong with me, not at work on a week day.

2. *We have been here a year*

and today I unpacked a box in the shed
labelled *shed*. Inside, the cycle helmets
from when the children were little, a squirrel
proof bird-feeder and elastic straps

for the roof-rack we had on the Volvo.
The Volvo – when Alan drove it out
of the compound it went on and on
and on the way home I called at a garage

because I couldn't switch off the lights.
It's a Volvo, they said. I collapsed
the handles of the lawnmower
to make more room in the shed.

Pilates

'You need some exercise,' my wife says.
'Besides, you won't be the only man there.'
Pilates Jane moves like a cat
in skin-tight black. The women flow,
positon to position, core muscles in place.
Gwilym's clattering arms and legs
are windmill blades, bent, unhinged.
He doesn't seem to notice. Brendan
grunts and strains. I'm knackered.
I don't get it. Men never do,
Jane confides. Brendan balances, topples,

bounces on the sprung floor. Again.
Again. I'm laughing so much I can
hardly breathe. Jane says something.
I turn over: 'Can't we just watch Brendan?'
In the car park he's on his phone.
Facebook. 'What are you saying, Brendan?
What are you telling the world?'

She's Living in Spain with Italians

If we had a dog it would be asleep
under the table after all the excitement.
Her first evening home and she's talking
with her mother in Italian, the Hotpoint
on slow wash and the birds out of hiding:
a baby tit head-butts the window, a fat thrush
fluffed out on the bench, a couple of dozy
wood pigeons on the fence checking out
the half-barrel pond outside the summer house.

We abandon the washing up and do a crazy dance
around the kitchen to Half Man Half Biscuit.
'It's better than what we called ourselves
when we formed a band.'
'What *did* you call yourselves?'
The dog at the patio door, ears back,
tail going, waiting to be let out
so it can chase the birds out of the garden.

Straw

He's in Barcelona, helping a bloke build a house.
'Mind you don't drop a brick on your foot.'
'He's not using bricks Dad, he's using straw.'

'Straw? Like the three pigs?' He laughs.
This bloke has a blind parrot on his shoulder.
'Like a pirate? You couldn't make this up.'

The parrot belongs to his ex-girlfriend
whose cat was after it. He lives on the hill.
They grow all their own food.

It used to be a leper colony.
I think he said leper colony.
He was tired. He had slept on the hill,

woke to a strange alarm from a bad dream.
The dream was with him as we spoke.

Lighthouse 2

She walked along the lighthouse beam
revolving under a blanked-out sky
in her bare feet and red dressing gown.

We watched from an upstairs window,
the smell of scorched vinyl
from the bonfire in the garden.

She was singing, her voice in front of her
leading her on as bats circled
and zig-zagged about the garden.

It was now, and that's all there ever will be:
her footsteps on light into the dark,
her voice. Night shivers as the clouds pass

and when the stars appear you think
you can see her among them, there –
a speck of red above the horizon.

Changing the Bed

Maybe it's unhooking the bottom sheet
and peeling it back, bundling it up
and throwing it in the corner
with the pillow cases; maybe
it's smoothing out the clean one
or finding the corners in the duvet cover
and shaking it between us,
or the competition of who's going to fasten
the most buttons which you always win;
maybe it's breathing in the freshness
with the window open and the sun
coming in to brighten the room and us.

Then we'll have a cup of tea and put our feet up

I'm at my mother's, on the stepladder
from Dad's old shed, clearing out the gutter
above the kitchen window with a garden trowel
and bucket in my 'new' overcoat,
ten pounds from the Islamic Charity Shop.

My mother, a tea towel on her shoulders
to keep off the rain, can't believe the amount
I'm digging out, of moss and gravel from the flat roof.
No wonder it's blocked. Leave the pots, she says,
she'll sweep up the leaves and then put them back.

It takes her forty-five minutes, she tells me later, on the phone.
'Thanks for all you did, it was a lovely afternoon.'

How do **you** *fly in your dreams?*

In dreams I leap like a man on the moon but higher
and further over fields and mountains and trees.
My wife does breast-stroke, if she stops she will sink
through the air. Our Luke flies sitting as if in the bath,
his legs in front of him, bent at the knees, moving
his hands like paddles. His girlfriend flies upright
as if in a lift. Our daughter floats in space with the stars.

Mum doesn't dream of flying, she dreams
of riding her bike. 'I rode a bike till I was eighty.'
She dreams of walking fast, of running.
She doesn't dream of flying, no,
she rides her bike, she runs, she climbs.

Gate

A gate, halfway up the garden,
a wrought iron gate she once painted cream
so that she could see it.

You could step around the gate,
if truth were told, there's plenty of room
on either side, but always

we walk through the gate, careful
not to latch it. Her fingers, at eighty-eight,
can no longer manage the latch

and her legs can barely manage the step.
'Mind you shut the gate,' she says,
as she always says, on the way back down,

turning round, just to make sure:
'Pull it to. Keep out the draught. That's it.'

Middle age is a walk through the woods
without your parents.
Your children have run ahead.
The sun is out, there are so many trees.

The End of the World Again

Dolphin Street, Port Isaac. It's raining.
Crab sandwiches and a pot of tea
in the café on the hill, now we're back
in the cottage under a duvet on the sofa;
I'm reading *Exit Music* from the shelf
I always bang my head on coming down the stairs,
we're sharing a box of Maltesers and wondering
why we have to drive all the way to Cornwall
and rent a cottage in order to live like kings.

Last night I dreamed it was the end
of the world again and I was about to give birth
from my right leg. The holy woman said:
*I want you to think of three things:
your mother, a potato and a disappointment.*
I couldn't think of a single disappointment.

Rain on the Conservatory Roof

First it rains, then it stops, then it rains
again. The blackbird hops on the lawn
with its keen eye, looking to be fed.
The wind chimes chime by the door,
the clocks tick in the clock-emptied house
and though the furniture's gone, its ghosts
are here: the drawers still full of her things,
the bed with the dent where she slept.

The mirror above her chair that's no longer there
reflects back all that the room has seen
and all that was said you can hear:
the sound of our voices when we first moved in
and I was as high as the window ledge
watching Dad painting the ceiling ...

Me and my brother cleaning the skirting
listen for our lives in the living room.

The House is Almost Empty

and all the things I might have kept are gone.
I've got the Christmas biscuit tin of candles
and the two and a half bottles of brandy
from the cupboard under the stairs.
I unscrew two hooks from the back of the door
and drop them in my bag with the horseshoes
that were nailed to the fence out the back
(I left the next people one) and the cartoon
key ring that the house keys were on.
I leave the dressing gown cord
on the back of her bedroom door.

Lighthouse 3

And then, stepping out onto the BEAM,
a white horse as if newly awake
or learning to walk again, stroking the light
with its hoof, unsure it will bear its weight,
wondering where brightness ends,
and night begins. Next on the BEAM
a procession: a ringmaster, brooding,
without a whip, out of his depth;
acrobats; the tightrope walker, rope
suspended, threaded through
the centre of the revolving BEAM;
the dawdling clown with bulging pockets,
looking over his shoulder, wheeling
a barrow – he stops, puts it down,
checks his watch and he's off again;
the gambler shuffles cards on the BEAM,
the dice rolling loud in the whites
of his eyes that snap into focus
(what does it mean when his eyes roll a six?)
hands of cards spill out of his pocket,
scatter, re-group, line up in the BEAM,
a royal flush disappears in the dark;
a man on a bike, an upright bike,
in a cap, a raincoat and bicycle clips,
you can almost hear his dynamo click,
chased by a dog, white in the BEAM
with a red collar, who runs much faster
than the man on the bike
but can not, cannot catch him.
The juggler next, who drops a plate
that does not smash on the BEAM
or splash in the sea, no sound but
the lingering song of the woman in red

and the music, seared, faded, released
from the vinyl, not so much music
as its memory, from embers and ash
cut loose, slipped free.

Everyone Took What They Wanted

Peg from next door in her overcoat
in the crowded living room, her back
to the fire in an upright chair, the pig

she has chosen from the garden under her arm,
sipping tea, eating a chocolate biscuit.
'Shall I take that for you Peg, put it by the front door?'

Diane has the bird table, Matty has the garden fork
and lawn rake, Alex has the fridge magnets
and Aunty Pam has the classical music CDs,

a book from the downstairs toilet and the picture
of the sheep in the mist above the mantelpiece:
'Your mum wanted me to have that.'

Peg next door says that when we were little
she would put her head in the cupboard
so that she could hear us laughing.

Travis Perkins

Me and Phil are at Travis Perkins
picking up some breathable
membrane. Ted is sorting us out.

'There's my mate down that hole,'
Ted says. The hole is in the car park
by a pile of rubble and a mini digger.

Ted's mate, in hi-vis, hard hat,
wrap-around sunglasses,
is up to his chest, shovelling

in the sunshine as if he's looking
for something. He's a big bloke,
he can barely fit. In fact the hole

is just the right size. He sees us.
'All right?' he says, and waves.

www.ingramcontent.com/pod-product-compliance
Lightning Source LLC
Chambersburg PA
CBHW051712040426
42446CB00008B/846